Overcoming The Pain of Infidelity

Camille K. Fender

OVERCOMING THE PAIN OF INFIDELITY.

Printed in the United States of America.

Light
PUBLISHERS

ISBN: 978-1-966723-47-9 (paperback)

Dedication and Acknowledgments

I dedicate this book with passion to my mother, Sandra (Peaches), who, with love and care, fought for me the best way she knew how. You were always there and went through every bit of pain, shame, and hardship with me. You showed up, not caring what others thought, but only focusing on what I was feeling because of your experiences. I love you, Mom.

Dwayne Fender, thank you. This is the Lord's doing.

To my dearly beloved children, Tawayne and Briana Fender. It was an experience we shared. I appreciate you so much. You warmed my heart with the little hugs and gave me hope with your smiles. You guys are amazing, and I pray that you will both be the man and woman God has destined you to be.

My Aunt Juliet (Mochie), you are an inspiration. Thank you for always standing by me.

Grandma (Gladys), you are unique and special; a grandmother who not only loves and cares for her own, but for all. Thank you for helping me understand the purpose and power of prayer. You are a champion.

Abigail, my one and only sister, as you grew and understood what was happening, you quickly fell into a defensive stance, ready to take on and take down anyone who tried to come near for a second. I love you, sis.

Kemar (Sticie), my brother, we grew together, cried together, and went through all the pain life brings during childhood and entering adulthood. Every time I got kicked out of the house, you came for me. Thank you, bro!

Auntie Jen, thank you, dear, for standing by me and staying for hours, comforting and being a friend, a mother, and a sister.

Nickeal, thank you for standing up for us and for believing that I would have overcome and be who God has called me to be. You never judged me, and you cared. Bless you always.

Mr. Chritooher Walker, thank you for showing up at the time needed most. God bless you.

Crystal Daye, thank you for your patience, for your obedience, and for never giving up on me. You are a gem, and I appreciate you always. Thank you, DayeLight Publishers, for the great work you have done as a team.

I give thanks to all the other special people who have contributed to my success. Pastor Gordon, his wife and family, Karen, Angela, Gabrielle, Miss Winsome, Jodi, Melissa, Racquel, and all others who have contributed greatly to my life.

Thank you. I believe every prayer, every laugh, every sad time, every good time, every telephone conversation, and every way you all supported me was just God. God used everyone strategically to help me endure until this day.

To my newborn Kawayne and Rawayne Fender, welcome, and you will become who God has called you to be.

Thank you all, and I love you!

Heavenly Father, I commit the person who is about to read into your hands.

As it is written in Psalm 37:5, "Commit thy way unto the Lord; trust also in him; and he shall bring it to pass." (KJV).

I pray for deliverance, change, and transformation, and for healing and restoration.
In Jesus' Name. Amen.

Preface

"Whether a woman has stayed, left, or been left, it must be remembered that time is the salve on this journey towards forgiveness and healing, because it is also a grieving process. The majority of women today have been deeply hurt through the act of infidelity, leaving them with scars and a deep sense of loss and grief from the betrayal." —Meryn G. Callandar

Infidelity is a traumatic experience that comes with ripple effects when you discover that your partner betrayed you. The shocking revelation leaves you numb and disoriented, raises many questions, and compels you to engage in introspection. Then you start to question yourself. *What? When did all of this happen? Why did he do this to me? What am I not doing? What does this other person have that I don't? When did he find the time for that? Oh no, how could I be so stupid? Am I not a good wife? Is this for real?*

The reality is, although you ask yourself these questions, you need these answers from him.

A myriad of emotions, such as doubt, anxiety, fear, and denial, will arrest you immediately and have you in a surrendered position until you realize that only God has all the answers to the questions. The question remains: *Should I stay in this marriage or leave?* The mental, emotional, financial, and physical process from this traumatic experience can take a lifetime if there is a void against how you truly feel about the betrayal. Working it out is not just with yourself and your partner, but also with the third person who came into the marriage. This can become more traumatic if, during the act of infidelity, a child comes into place.

"Overcoming The Pain of Infidelity" focuses on the circumstances that married women are faced with when they discover that their husband had an affair with another woman. The hurt is deeper when the other woman becomes pregnant, and a child is also involved. Denial, depression, brokenness, neglect, anger, shame, bitterness, and anxiety make it harder to accept the truth. Forgiveness and relearning to love again are challenging. Forgiveness is the primary objective because it is one of the major factors preventing you from living a purposeful life as you progress through the marriage.

Through discussions and interviews, I have discovered that many women are walking around with deep wounds in their souls from previous and present hurts that stemmed from infidelity, leaving them sick within their bodies, souls, and minds.

As a woman who has experienced the act of infidelity, I went through a state of abandonment. I was physically, emotionally, sexually, verbally, and mentally abused to the point where it affected me psychologically. Being so aware of the effects of infidelity has led me to identify that many women are going around with deep wounds from previous and present hurts that stemmed from this cruel act.

This book is a firsthand account of what I went through and how God helped me overcome the pain. Through this book, I hope to inspire you to reclaim your true self, let go of shame, find the strength to forgive, and live a meaningful life.

"For I will restore health unto thee, and I will heal thee of thy wounds, saith the LORD; because they called thee an Outcast, saying, this is Zion, whom no man seeketh after." (Jeremiah 30:17 - KJV).

"Call unto me, and I will answer thee, and show thee great and mighty things, which thou knowest not." (Jeremiah 33:3 - KJV).

Table of Contents

Introduction

What is Infidelity?

According to Merriam-Webster, infidelity is the act of having a romantic or sexual relationship with someone other than one's husband or wife.

I extend grace if you choose to leave the marriage after the act of infidelity and do it all over again with someone else. However, you can be healed from the pain of infidelity, forgive, and restore your relationship with your spouse.

Within the first year of being married, I discovered that my husband was cheating with another woman, and to exacerbate the situation, the woman (side chick) lived within the same community and got pregnant with a child for my husband. I was devastated. I felt like I was in a 3D movie, and life abruptly ended, and our relationship took a dramatic turn for the worse. With the many questions and wonderings, I became clinically depressed for years. I would have never imagined that one day the pain would end, my family would be restored, and I would be able to love my husband again and live a meaningful life.

God's intent for man is to become one flesh with his wife. As stated in *Genesis 2:22-24, "And the rib, which the Lord God had taken from man, made he a woman, and brought her unto the man. And Adam said, This is now bone of my bones, and flesh of my flesh: she shall be called Woman, because she was taken out of Man. Therefore shall a man leave his father and his mother, and shall cleave unto his wife: and they shall be one flesh." (KJV).* Also, in the book of Mark 10:8-9, we see where Jesus Christ solidifies man and woman to marry and become one flesh. Consequently, in the book of 1 Samuel, the story of Hannah and Peninnah is used to encapsulate how infidelity can cause serious family problems.

Chapter 1

Until It Knocks at Your Door

"Love suffers long and is kind; love does not envy; love does not parade itself, is not puffed up; does not behave rudely, does not seek its own, is not provoked, thinks no evil; does not rejoice in iniquity, but rejoices in the truth; bears all things, believes all things, hopes all things, endures all things." (1 Corinthians 13:4-7 - KJV).

The Bible speaks explicitly about love, and so it is: when a man and a woman establish their love for each other, the next step is usually marriage.

Whoso findeth a wife findeth a good thing and obtained favour from the Lord. (Proverbs 18:22 – KJV).

People tend to get married based on religious beliefs, cultural norms, and tradition; so, people get married because they might grow up in a Christian home that teaches that sex outside of marriage is fornication. To avoid damaging their relationship with God, they might just enter into a marriage to fulfill their desires. The scripture states: *"But if they cannot contain, let them marry: for it is better to marry than to burn." (1 Corinthians 7:9 – KJV).*

This is usually stressed on by believers in Christian homes and taken out of context, which pressures young believers to get married before they are truly prepared.

Tradition and culture share an interconnectedness with specific beliefs that if someone is not married at a particular age, they are scoffed at, and society sees the woman as undesirable to men. This puts pressure on the woman to just accept anything about anyone. It is critically important that ample time be given for persons to understand the true essence of God's will concerning marriage, rather than feeling pressured or compelled to get married out of fear.

Consequently, when a man gets on his knees and asks, *"Will you marry me?",* rather than taking time to reflect on the state of the relationship and carefully consider their decision, we get butterflies, become overwhelmed, anxious, and hastily make the announcement. With immediate effect, we will commence planning and preparing for that special day. Interestingly, for most women, the day of their wedding is probably the sweetest day of their life because it is on this day that they put out every effort to show up looking like a princess, as in the fairytale movies. Women invest time getting dolled up to show up, give their spouse a sense of awe, and be celebrated by all their families and friends.

Grooms typically maintain a calm demeanor to ensure they meet their bride's expectations. Wow, all this preparation is intended for a happily ever after. While it is okay for everyone to have their dream wedding, it would be more beneficial to focus on getting proper guidance on what we should expect in marriage. The days and months spent on all this preparation can easily become a nightmare in one minute of making a poor decision. Before you know it, infidelity knocks at your door and turns your world upside down.

Infidelity is a pandemic, and the virus is on the rise, affecting marriages over the years, and sadly, it is normalised by society. Through observations and conversation, it is the belief of most women that marital infidelity should remain confidential. Often, when a man is unfaithful to his wife, the woman is expected to stay quiet as a way of giving respect and protecting her home. Once again, the scripture is used out of context: *"For the husband is the head of the wife, even as Christ is the head of the church: and he is the saviour of the body. Therefore as the church is subject unto Christ, so let the wives be to their own husbands in every thing." (Ephesians 5:23-24 – KJV).*

This is usually used to substantiate the act of silence. Remembering how in-depth this scripture was used to explain how a wife should honor her husband humbly, despite, I smile. Because when infidelity knocks at your door, everything changes.

When I met my husband, I was baptized and actively involved in church. Our relationship started as friends for two years. Our interest began to spark, and we decided to show care for each other because we were convinced that we were meant for each other. Immensely, our relationship as friends felt safe and secure as we walked each other through the good and bad times, as two young people not knowing much and not having the support of parents, friends, and siblings, as we should. He would attend church with me often, and one day, surprisingly, he accepted the Lord and was baptized. I was not even there because the decision he made for himself was that much of a surprise. This caused me to gravitate to him even more, and after a while, we decided to be more than just friends.

I thought we waited long enough, and we started having sex, and not long after, I got pregnant. I did not accept, nor did I want to believe, so I went to the doctor, and it was confirmed that I was pregnant. This was a scary moment for me because I was a church girl who sang on the choir and never missed a service for no reason at all. At twenty-one years of age, my life shifted in a direction I didn't understand, and I did not know how to face my mom. I knew this would have been devastating for her, given all she was already going through. Not to mention how ashamed I felt as a Christian girl within my community and how I would be viewed, along with the accusation that is generally given to the church. The fact is, sex out of marriage, according to the Word of God, is a sin, and there is no way around that. Fornication is viewed as a "BIG" sin.

The first person I told was my brother, with whom I shared a very close relationship. He was that type of brother who loved and cared very much for me, and as a result, he did the same towards my husband. So, he was the one who took it up as an initiative to break the news and tell my mom, because, as men, even though he was in church as well, they didn't see the big deal. For them, it was just life; things happen, and we are only human.

One morning, my brother decided he was going to Mom's room to tell her, and I stayed in the other room and waited. After he did, she called me to her room and asked, *Is it true?* In fear, I responded, *"Yes."* She cried for a moment and then expressed her anger and disappointment. I was so sad, but my husband and brother were extremely happy, and with every effort, they gave me all the love, care, and support that I needed for that moment and throughout the journey. In those moments, I saw my husband as the man for me. He took very good care of me, and I cannot remember when I needed him or something, and it was not provided, so throughout my pregnancy, despite all that was happening around me with the slanders, criticisms, and how ashamed I felt, his care and love towards me created an environment of love. My parents, siblings, and other relatives were proud of how he responded and stood by me. That took away the shame and reproach during that time. According to 1 Peter 4:8, love covers a multitude of sins. I was convinced even more that this was my life partner, and nothing could change my mind. I didn't understand that there was a deeper side to a relationship than just providing and caring for the person.

As I mentioned, so much was happening with my mom. My parents were married but did not have a healthy marriage; our home was dysfunctional, and abuse was highly prevalent. My dad provided financially and ensured the bills were paid; however, infidelity and abuse were the order of the day, and when he came home, there was no peace. Quarrels and physical fights were continuous. So, now that I was pregnant, even though my mom was not in agreement, I was happy because I would be free to go to my husband's house and stay there to be at peace and away from the noise. It was easy for me because his parents and siblings treated me respectfully and cared for me very well.

Time went by so fast, and I gave birth to our son. It was one of the most joyful times in our lives and the family. With our newborn baby, the start of a new life for us as parents had just begun, and we were managing the best way we understood. Also, the support and love from both sides of the family were extended to us as we nurtured and grew our child between homes.

Fast forward two years, and I discovered I was now pregnant again with a second child for my husband. I remember this like yesterday because my husband was so excited again. After all, he said he was confident this would be a girl. I was there panicking and thinking how I allowed this to happen again because I was so comfortable with my new life, and everything was going well. I went to the doctor, and it was confirmed that I was pregnant. I was sad and felt like an unworthy Christian, feeling bad because I just could not please God. I expressed to my husband how I felt, and the following week, he proposed and asked me to marry him. I was not ready, and I was confused and scared. Still, wanting to honor God's Word, escape the shame, and get away from the dysfunctional home that seemed to be getting worse and not better, I accepted. As a church girl, not getting the love of my father, who, whenever he came home, it was pure quarreling and fights, and to avoid my mom from the stress and worrying about what people would say, I said yes. So, we decided to get married as soon as possible, get on with our lives, have our own family, and create a healthy environment to raise our children.

We informed our parents, and they gave us their blessings. We started with our planning for that special day. As we got closer to the time, and while planning, I began to have off-feelings, but because of my early stage of pregnancy, I ignored the feelings, thinking it was related to my pregnancy. I wanted to align myself with the Word of God, move forward, and create the family I wanted. In April 2007, we got married, and I gave birth to our beautiful daughter in October 2007.

After we got married, we moved in together because we were going back and forth between my home and his. Things were going well: his sister moved in with us to help because I was not doing so well with a sickness that stemmed from my pregnancy, and my husband was away working out of town. But the joy and peace I once felt with us were gone, and I started having weird dreams. For months, I dreamt of two lizards: one living in our bedroom over the bed we slept on, and the other at the entrance. I did not understand that these were visions and God was showing me what was happening. I then noticed that my husband was no longer communicating with me as usual, especially when he was working far away from home. When he came home, everything about him was different. He no longer wanted to be around, so the love and support I needed, being pregnant, was not given. I was neglected, and it made me angry, broken, sad, and "miserable." We started quarrelling a lot, and I became suspicious of his silent phone. I took it upon myself to search the phone and noticed a specific number repeatedly as his main contact every day, which was very often. I asked questions about the number and who the person was. It made him angry, and not long after, I discovered who the girl was. That was when I realized something had gone wrong. I did not know what to do or how to respond, so I started to answer based on how I saw my mother respond. *Children live what they learn*. It made matters worse because now it was an excuse for him not to come home, as with our culture, *"When a woman is miserable, the man stays away."*

The Nightmare

After the discovery, my husband's behaviour grew worse and became a nightmare. I felt like I was being crushed slowly but surely. The intense pressure mentally, physically, and emotionally led to "premature birth." When I was in labour, he took me to the hospital gate, dropped me off, and wished me "Good Luck." I walked into the hospital in pain, broken in pieces.

I called Mom, crying. I asked her to come, and she and my grandmother came. They were in shock after I explained what had happened. They could not believe it, but we pressed through together that day, focusing on my well-being and giving birth to my child. After I was discharged from the hospital, with all that was happening, I stayed at my mom's home for a long time to be cared for, and he hardly came around. To make matters even worse, on the day of our daughter's christening, he never showed up. This now led back to the same young lady, who I now started to get phone calls from, giving me the alarm that infidelity was knocking at my door.

So, my husband, with whom I had a fairytale wedding, became unfaithful to me with another woman who lived a stone's throw away from me. To make it worse, he impregnated her. I found out on the day she called multiple times, and I got frustrated and went by the shop where she worked to tell her to stop calling my phone. She said, *"Dutty bitch, me a breed fi yuh husband, and I hope him tell yuh because yuh affi live wid it."* This was another series of nightmares for me, my children, and my family. She was never humble, and to add to her behaviour, her mother, sister, my husband, my husband's family, his sister, who lived with me, and most of the people within the community took her side. This was normal behaviour and lifestyle for them, so I was the odd one and was seen as the enemy because I decided I would not accept it.

Almost every day, when I stepped out of my house to do anything, she was there mocking me, jeering me, throwing words at me, laughing at me, and, to make it worse, this was done when she was sitting at a corner shop where she worked for my husband's older sister, who would also be there along with others laughing. If I were coming from church, she would wait along the road with her mother and sister, and they would walk behind me with the children, and the mockery would go on. They would laugh and make fun of me, saying, *"Walk up wid di fender baby in a yuh belly."* If I were home and came outside to do anything around the house, she was next door with my husband, siblings, and their wives mocking, jeering, and laughing. So, I had no peace in the community, and my husband would quarrel with me and reject me in every way he could.

Time passed, and she gave birth in October 2008. Her child was now born within the same community next door to our matrimonial home, in my face. Infidelity knocked at my door and entered. I felt as if my life ended abruptly, and our marriage in seconds took a dramatic turn downhill.

Life happens. I was devastated to the point where I just wanted to end my life. It was one of the most painful experiences, and it affected me mentally, physically, emotionally, and even financially. It did not just affect me, but all areas of my life, directly and indirectly, including my loved ones, pulling us worlds apart. Our children were especially seriously affected.

I was dying slowly but surely with intense pain on the inside. Showing up and showing off were my priorities, more than asking for help or expressing my anger, bitterness, hatred, distrust, loss of hope, confidence, and self-esteem. I battered myself with pride trying to save my marriage and husband to avoid the shame and failure, leading to a state of insanity: *"The mad woman in clean clothes was Camille."* I lost my identity. Infidelity slapped me right in the face with no compassion, empathy, or sympathy. The pain of infidelity is costly. I tried to fight my battles and save my husband more than myself. The Word of God gave me hope and released me from the guilt I felt, as if I had made one of the biggest mistakes.

Marriage is honourable in all, and the bed undefiled: but whoremongers and adulterers God will judge. (Hebrews 13:4 – KJV).

This verse helped build my hope and trust in God because of all the different adversaries, feelings, doubt, fear, disbelief, questions, and accusations. This scripture gave hope and reminded me that God is fighting for me.

Infidelity is a pandemic. It can take you by surprise, causing many changes within and in your life. It will affect you mentally, physically, and emotionally, leaving you in a state of wonder with many questions. *Why?* It can cause you to become worried and concerned, shifting your focus, and before you know it, it is confirmed, and you now have to make necessary adjustments in all areas of your life. Yes, this is how infidelity causes us to feel; it has a ripple effect within all areas of our lives. You will feel like you are in a 3D movie. It increases your heartbeat, making you wonder what's happening. You become dysfunctional, and all you will find yourself doing is asking questions, wanting answers. However, the cases of infidelity are without fail and deeply rooted, distinctive, spiritual, and occasionally dangerous to the point of causing death in some cases. Does it give warnings? Yes! Some are noticeable, some aren't, and by the time you decide to pay attention and take action, it is already at your door. These gestures are normal when faced with a crisis. It can be very daring, especially when it wasn't just a "one-night stand," but a long-standing relationship with an old friend, your best friend, a relative of yours, your sister, or a neighbour.

Let's Examine The Affliction of Hannah from Her Adversary, Peninnah

"And her adversary also provoked her sore, for to make her fret, because the LORD had shut up her womb. And as he did so year by year, when she went up to the house of the LORD, so she provoked her; therefore she wept, and did not eat." (1 Samuel 1:6-7 - KJV).

When you read the entire chapter of 1 Samuel 1, the story of Hannah and Peninnah is a perfect example. However, it was common for men to have more than one wife, and the marriage culture was one where a woman's value was based on her ability to bear a child. Barrenness was seen as not just personal but a public shame, especially within their culture. The narrative states that Elkanah had two wives, Hannah and Peninnah, but that Peninnah had children while Hannah had none. Regardless of their culture, Hannah was genuinely disturbed by her adversary, Peninnah, who provoked and insulted her daily.

To the woman reading, you have been insulted by your adversary and may feel genuinely pressured with fear, self-worth, and shame, unworthiness, dishonour, disrespect, self-pity, loss, betrayal, insecurity, hurt, anger, regret, guilt, anxiety, depression, and low self-esteem, and your heart may be sinking. You may be afraid to let the tears out. You do not want others to see; you want to show strength. You fear expressing yourself and feelings around your friends and loved ones because you do not want them to look down on you or think you are weak. You may be wondering what is going to happen, but it is okay. Infidelity knocked at your door and caused you pain.

Hannah wept and did not eat; I wept and did not eat. It is okay and a part of the processing. It does not matter what the belief is, what culture or religion says, when infidelity shows up at your door, it is only the grace of God that will carry you through this valley, if you allow Him. God is in your midst, and you shall not be moved. This is not the end of your destiny. The journey has just started. Infidelity knocked at your door unexpectedly in a way that you least expected it. Some shut the door in its face with denial as quickly as possible to suppress the feelings, while others have opened their doors and allowed it to come in and find rest, leaving you unsettled.

The race is not for the swift nor the battle for the strong but for him who endures until the end (see Ecclesiastes 9:11). When infidelity knocks at your door, it is meant to kill you, but trust God, for what the enemy meant for evil, God will turn around for good. Rise above the pain of infidelity and overcome because you are destined. Manipulate your pain for a purpose as I take you on the journey of overcoming infidelity after it knocks at your door.

REWRITE THESE SCRIPTURES AS A DECLARATION AND PERSONALIZE THEM

And he said unto me, My grace is sufficient for thee: for my strength is made perfect in weakness. Most gladly therefore will I rather glory in my infirmities, that the power of Christ may rest upon me. (2 Corinthians 12:9 – KJV).

____

____

____

____

Dearly beloved, avenge not yourselves, but rather give place unto wrath: for it is written, Vengeance is mine; I will repay saith the Lord. (Romans 12:19 – KJV).

Chapter 2

It Is Not A Shame, So Break The Silence

Shame is an emotion that arises after a person makes a choice that does not align with their values. They may believe they made this poor choice because something is inherently wrong with them. These negative and self-critical internal judgments can leave many feeling inadequate or unworthy of being loved.

I have never felt so ashamed in my entire life; my self-esteem was extremely damaged, and I felt worthless, inadequate, and started to have a negative self-image. I was withdrawn socially for a long time because I struggled with trust, depression, anxiety, and anger, trying to mask my pain. The shame of being a victim of infidelity had me trapped in a dark place. To be told publicly by another woman, *"I am pregnant with a child for your husband, and you have to accept it,"* silenced me, causing dysfunction in the way I show up and behave as a person, especially the more I internalized it. It made me feel like I had made the worst decision in my life because all odds seemed to be against me, which made me think I was making a big deal, especially with the constant encounters and word-throwing related to why my husband cheated. I felt as if I had no voice. As a church girl, I was encouraged only to pray and leave it to God. I would go to church, sing, have the time of my life, hastily go home, lock my doors, and cry. Everyone had something to say, but when I spoke, it always seemed as if I was a disgrace to myself, my children, and my family. So, between home, the other woman, and the community were quarrels, criticisms, and a lot of saying, but I was expected to stay silent.

I sought Christian counseling professionally, and it did not help because it was centered on me doing what was expected based on culture, tradition, and religion to do all that is to be done for the benefit of the "head" of the house. I stopped because it was not making any sense, and it was only making me more silent.

The more I kept silent, the more I became agitated, leading to what I had been avoiding: a dysfunctional home. Things worsened the more I spoke out, and because I was now heard. I became a problem, and one Sunday morning, my in-laws—joined by others—came by and chased me away, all because I started responding to my husband, and they knew because we all lived on their family land. My husband and I quarreled so often that at times I felt ashamed. This was a tough moment in my life. I cried until there were no tears left inside. These were the consequences of breaking free from silence.

Let us face it: most of us grew up in dysfunctional homes. A dysfunctional home is characterized by "conflict, misbehavior, or abuse," where the relationships among family members within the household can be marked by neglect, yelling, and screaming. Also, many of us are witnesses of domestic violence/abuse that stemmed from a dysfunctional home. Domestic violence/abuse is a pattern of abusive behavior in any relationship that is used by one partner to gain or maintain power and control over another intimate partner. Domestic violence can be physical, sexual, emotional, economic, psychological, or technological actions or threats of actions or other patterns of coercive behavior that influence another person within an intimate relationship. This includes behaviors that intimidate, manipulate, humiliate, isolate, frighten, terrorize, coerce, threaten, blame, hurt, injure, or wound someone. However, it is evident that the main source of these problems stems from "infidelity."

These types of behaviors provoked by infidelity in marriages within the home are so common that they force you to happily accept negative treatment as normal. This gives you no open space to express your thoughts and feelings freely, with the belief that "man and woman," especially those married, problems are private matters or "big people arguments." Some will say, *"Mi nah get inna man and woman argument because by later a de two a dem a put head pon pillar."* However, from my experiences, the time at which others start withdrawing from marital infidelity happens when the wife discovers the truth and all those who contributed to the problems. Most people withdraw in fear, and for the most part, to respect privacy.

Women are the main victims of these situations. Because of the withdrawal of others, especially loved ones, and as I mentioned earlier, because of cultural norms, tradition, and religious belief, they have been silent under the weather of infidelity. It has been affecting them mentally, physically, and emotionally, causing them to live a lie and a deceitful life. So, as a veteran from a dysfunctional home, one who faced infidelity and domestic violence, I must say it is not a private matter. It is not a shame so break the silence. It is not a secret, neither is it a "man and woman thing"; it is a worldwide pandemic that has taken root within marriages over years and should be addressed openly. The Word of God says: *"There is a way which seemeth right unto a man, but the end thereof are the ways of death." (Proverbs 14:12 - KJV).*

In this verse, we can relate and admit that staying silent seems to be the right way, but the truth is that silence leads to death, emotionally, physically, and spiritually.

- Emotionally, women become numb and disconnected from their emotions.

- Physically, women develop sicknesses caused by stress or have encounters that cause fights, leading to permanent death.
- Spiritually, some women blame God, avoid praying, attending church, and participating in activities that contribute to their spiritual life.

It is very dangerous in situations of infidelity because silence is a decision to allow anything to come our way and have its way.

Breaking The Silence

Firstly, let's discuss breaking the silence by seeking out people you can trust to discuss the situation. Talking to people you can trust and who can relate to how you feel will help you connect, feel safe, provide guidance, reduce stress, negative thinking, loneliness, and emotional distress, and provide opportunities for perspective-sharing. The more you talk about it, the better you will feel.

Jesus lived as a perfect example by choosing His twelve disciples whom He could relate to, and everywhere He went, He addressed anything contrary to what His Father says assertively, using the Word, the power, and the authority given to Him. So, all we need is a circle or a community of like-minded women who can relate to help us through the pandemic of infidelity. Many women have kept their mouths shut, and the pain of infidelity has caused them to die on the bed of affliction: sad, broken, angry, bitter, unfulfilled, and with a loss of identity. They left behind a legacy of generational curse, negative patterns, and battles for their children to fight. There is a saying that *"A good friend is better than pocket money."* Ten minutes of sharing laughter is much healthier than one minute of pain and grief.

When I was going through the pain of infidelity, at first, I would stay locked at home and cry as much as I could before the kids got home. When I went out to do anything, I would put on a lot of makeup to show up and make it seem okay, but I was not. Everyone in my community already knew what was happening. The only people I would talk to were my mom, aunt, and grandmother, and it did not help much, because they too had been constantly dealing with different episodes of infidelity within their marriages over the years. When I finished talking, I felt more burdened with the belief that if I should openly share, I would be a disgrace to myself and only be *"carrying down my husband."*

I would go to the hairdresser, and people who knew me and were aware of the situation would often start conversations. They would ask questions to see how I was coping and then share how they felt about the problem. Also, they shared how they would have dealt with it, seeing that the other woman was so presumptuous. This allowed me to open up and helped me realise that others disagreed with this behaviour away from my community. It was during these moments that these women shared that they too had experienced infidelity, expressed their anger, and discussed coping mechanisms. I then realised that out of every ten women, at least eight had the same experience. However, my encounter was so close and in my face, and that amazed them because they thought, *"Girl, you're strong cause I would probably go to jail already."* So, this caused me to start opening up as I realized that outside of my community, others had different views and were in total disagreement. These conversations helped break my silence, and going to the hairdresser became my weekly getaway.

Each day started to feel a little better, and the more I shared and laughed at the crazy moments and encounters, the more I felt empowered. There is nothing like sharing a space with women who care and give their support. Those ladies had no idea how therapeutic it was for me to come out and engage in those interactive moments.

My hairdresser, whom I admired as she showed strength even through her divorce and how she openly spoke about it, gave me hope. It made me realise that I was not alone, and staying silent would only keep me in a fragile state. Too many of us remain quiet for too long, so we lose ourselves along the way. Some women died because they chose to keep everything inside, resulting in poor decisions made from vulnerability, leaving them with regrets. Too many women have died in the battle of infidelity because they chose to stay quiet, allowing the enemy to use the darts from the situation to destroy them. I thought that staying silent was the right approach. However, after these experiences, I realised that arrogance is based on how culture and religion have shaped our minds. It's a myth.

"Open rebuke is better than secret love. Faithful are the wounds of a friend; but the kisses of an enemy are deceitful. The full soul loatheth an honeycomb; but to the hungry soul every bitter thing is sweet. As a bird that wandereth from her nest, so is a man that wandereth from his place." (Proverbs 27:5-8 – KJV).

God has given us the power, and He is our defense. The Word of God encourages us to be bold and courageous: *"Have I not commanded thee? Be strong and of a good courage; be not afraid, neither be thou dismayed: for the Lord thy God is with thee whithersoever thou goest." (Joshua 1:9 – KJV).*

Boldness, along with resilience, courage, and determination, will help you break the silence and be free. Apostle Selman stated in one of his sermons that, *"A closed mouth is a closed destiny."* Your voice is an access code in the realm of the Spirit and a key element that can be used strategically.

"Fear thou not; for I am with thee: be not dismayed; for I am thy God: I will strengthen thee; yea, I will help thee; yea, I will uphold thee with the right hand of my righteousness." (Isaiah 41:10 - KJV).

"Thou shalt also decree a thing, and it shall be established unto thee: And the light shall shine upon thy ways." (Job 22:28 - KJV).

"Death and life are in the power of the tongue: And they that love it shall eat the fruit thereof." (Proverbs 18:21 - KJV).

In addition, pray. Prayer changes things. It is the common denominator that we need to use in every situation: marriage/prayer, husband/prayer, side chicks/prayer, in-laws/prayer, negative friends/prayer, and the list goes on. Engaging in strategic prayer will give you that one-on-one time to talk to God about the situation. So, outside of our community to help cheer us on, invite God in the midst. Cast all your cares on God.

"Casting all your care upon him; for he careth for you." (1 Peter 5:7 - KJV).

Trust Him to take you through this season of your life and to surround you with the right people to overcome the fear and break the silence. God ordained marriage, and He honors it; it sets the foundation and tone of the home and the life of your children.

In honor of the late Dr. Myles Munroe, while listening to him teach on marriages, he stated these profound words: *"Marriage and its affairs are not secret because when we are getting married, we invite all our loved ones to come and be witnesses and celebrate with us, and so for this reason we owe it to all our loved ones to let them know what's happening."* I agree.

Infidelity is a public affair with two people outside the marriage in the eyes of everyone. Most of the time, the last person to know of the affair or affairs outside the marriage is the wife. Wives should not lock away their feelings of guilt and show pity while allowing these behaviors to deplete the original structure of marriage and the family concerning the Word of God. I saw the women I loved and who should have been role models suffer from the pain of infidelity, and as a result, fail to function effectively. However, I grew up and, through my own experiences, realised that someone had to break the silence because the same thing that happened to my grandmother, mother, and aunts was now happening to me, and I decided it would not happen to my children. This is where it stops. I had to silence the everyday whispers, complaints, misery, and sadness caused by infidelity. No one wanted to openly speak about it and get the needed help.

It is not a shame, and we will not be the first or the last to have this experience. It is not easy, and feeling ashamed is a part of the process. However, walking around feeling shame should not be a burden you carry. Break the silence, and do not let it suffocate you. Confess, confront, consult, be cautious, and take courage.

REWRITE THE SAME SCRIPTURES AS A DECLARATION AND PERSONALIZE THEM.

"Concerning this thing I pleaded with the Lord three times that it might depart from me. And He said to me, "My grace is sufficient

for you, for My strength is made perfect in weakness." Therefore most gladly I will rather boast in my infirmities, that the power of Christ may rest upon me. Therefore I take pleasure in infirmities, in reproaches, in needs, in persecutions, in distresses, for Christ's sake. For when I am weak, then I am strong." (2 Corinthians 12:8-10 - NKJV).

Chapter 3

Forgive Yourself

"Forgive yourself for not knowing better at the time. Forgive yourself for giving away your power. Forgive yourself for past behaviors. Forgive yourself for the survival patterns and traits you picked up while enduring trauma. Forgive yourself for being who you needed to be." —Bria Rivello

I strongly agree with Rivello because we did only what we knew how best to do. Forgiveness is freedom, and I believe the first stage of forgiveness starts with oneself. Forgiveness is an intentional decision to let go of resentment and anger.

After breaking the silence by sharing how I felt about everything happening, the different feedback took a toll on me. Some were positive, but others had negative input based on the situation. To add, after hearing all the stated reasons why I was cheated on by the other woman, it made it even worse, in addition to the behaviour of my husband. Sitting with myself and meditating on everything said, I felt guilty and sorry for myself. I struggled mentally processing it all and started blaming myself. As time went by, I found that I was becoming unhappier, with feelings of shame, guilt, self-acceptance, bitterness, and anger towards myself as an individual. After breaking the silence, I thought I would be in a better place mentally and emotionally. Then I realised that "Overcoming The Pain of Infidelity" is a process that takes time, and there are different stages to overcoming and living a meaningful life.

I started to withdraw from the noise again, as I did when I found out I was now a victim of infidelity and was openly embarrassed. It was now the talk of the town. I became so stressed, my physical health started to deteriorate, with constant headaches, pain all over my body, to the point where I could not sit up properly. I was unable to care for my children as I should, causing them to become sickly too. My trust in others had broken down, and I failed to move forward and maintain healthy relationships to help me navigate that season of my life. I was trapped in self-recrimination.

I battled with myself for ten years. I felt like I was going crazy—out of my mind—trying to figure out what was happening and why everyone was so distant from me and me from them. I encountered people who wanted to help, but I would not accept them. I had many failures in jobs, school, and other things I tried to do to uplift myself. But I failed because for the most I was only trying to get away and take my mind off the situation. Going into the 11th year, I got the prompt to move out of the community and the matrimonial home, and start again. I felt peace when I heard that still small voice, so I immediately went forward and made the necessary preparation. I informed only a few people who were standing by me. I found a place to rent and had to leave my children with my mom for a while. Leading up to the day I would go—about a week before I left—I told my husband I was leaving. I never wanted to say anything to him, but a good friend of mine advised me to inform him because he was the father of my children. This was hard because I wanted to just leave without notifying him and get on with my life. I humbled myself anyways, and I told him, and he responded humbly and decided to come with me. So, we left behind a vast house and relocated to a small house far away. I took nothing with me; to this day, all my clothes and other stuff are still locked up. Wow! This part felt easy, and I was at peace; this was how I knew it was the Lord's doing. This took me back to the story of Abraham in Genesis 12, when the Lord called Abraham and told him to leave his country and go to a land He would show him.

Now that I had relocated and started working, I started to feel better and more motivated. We also began attending a church in the area. The first time I stepped into the church, the worshippers sang "Made A Way" by Travis Greene, and the sermon was aligned that day. God ministered through His servant, and I listened. Time passed, and I started to feel a conviction to seek help. I asked to speak with the church's pastor and was given an appointment. When I went, His wife came to see me while I was waiting in the room and asked,

"Young Lady, how can I assist?" She explained that the pastor, her husband, was in a meeting and apologized as He would not be able to speak with me. I shared with her what was happening and how I was genuinely inspired upon visiting the church. I remembered how she smiled and answered, *"My dear, it sounds to me like God has taken you to a hospital so that He can heal you."* I stared at her for a moment, and she said, *"Let me break it down. With all that you shared, you are like a sick patient who has to be admitted to the hospital for treatment. God has admitted you by relocating you so that He can give you all the medication needed."* She then said it was a blessed evening and walked away. I left pondering and meditating on what she said for weeks.

I started paying more attention to my actions, how I responded to my husband, and how I felt about myself. I realised that the feelings were still there. Especially when I remembered the other woman and all the people who contributed to the situation. I grew worse, even though I was no longer in the environment.

I went to church, and a sermon on forgiveness was preached. The preacher made an altar call for those with unforgiveness to come, so I went. After leaving and going home, as time passed, I felt pressured to forgive him and others, especially when I was encouraged to do so from a biblical perspective. But then I realised I was pressured to forgive everyone except myself. When I realised how it made me feel, I had to sit, self-reflect, and identify the things I was struggling with. I then realised that I needed to forgive myself before I could forgive anyone else.

During this time of self-reflection, I realised I had a lot of work to do. I had to take the time to forgive myself of the guilt for not knowing better, for not seeking God, for deciding to get married as a get away from a dysfunctional home, forgive myself for having too much expectation from my husband, forgive myself for not being there for my children and for failing in the many ways I did that caused a significant setback in my life. I had to forgive myself for being too hard on myself to achieve a perfect, successful life. It was the best thing I did for myself. I forgave myself and decided to let go, let God, and move forward. In doing so, I realised that many things started to change. The changes caused me to start showing up differently and respond in a way that shows maturity.

Sister, I wonder why everyone puts pressure on wives to forgive everyone else but not themselves. When one masters the heart of forgiving oneself, intimacy begins. Forgiving yourself will set you free, cause you to see yourself for who you are, and bring you closer to God. Many people continue to struggle with forgiving others because they are in the prison of unforgiveness with themselves. Imagine being tied with a rope and trying to stretch out to save someone else.

When a man cheats, the wife is not meeting his needs; yes, 95% blame is on the wife. As a result, we join and blame ourselves with the given reasons and end up sabotaging ourselves: unforgiveness. We ask, *"Why should I forgive myself?"* Unforgiveness is a prison that will keep the pain alive, keep you in your past, and inhibit you. Of course, our actions can contribute to our spouses' unfaithfulness, but this does not give them the right to cheat on us. So, let us take responsibility for our actions and forgive ourselves.

The secret to overcoming unforgiveness is forgiving yourself first. Once you become free from the prison of unforgiveness, which had you locked up with shame, anger, bitterness, guilt, and self-acceptance, you will start experiencing its benefits. It will promote healthy relationships, self-compassion, forgiveness towards others, break you free from your past, increase your self-esteem, self-trust, resilience, learning, growth, enhance your productivity, and overall well-being.

God wants us to forgive ourselves because He has already forgiven us.

"For God so loved the world, that he gave his only begotten Son, that whosoever believeth in him should not perish, but have everlasting life." (John 3:16 – KJV).

God gave His Son to die for our sins that we may be forgiven.

"He will turn again, he will have compassion upon us; he will subdue our iniquities; and thou wilt cast all their sins into the depths of the sea." (Micah 7:19 – KJV).

Take your time and be very gentle with yourself as you go through forgiving yourself. It doesn't matter who you are, as stated in John 3:16, *"whosoever believeth,"* which means who you are, where you are from, what you have done, or who your parents are, or the background you come from doesn't matter. God forgives you before you even sin. So, whatever accusations make you feel unworthy, rise above them.

REWRITE THE SAME SCRIPTURES AS A DECLARATION AND PERSONALIZE THEM

Repent ye therefore, and be converted, that your sins may be blotted out, when the times of refreshing shall come from the presence of the Lord. (Acts 3:19 – KJV).

____

____

____

____

____

The Word of God encourages us to repent, that is, to turn away from our sins, and commit to Him so He can restore us and surround us with His presence.

Chapter 4

Forgive Your Husband

- Why should I forgive him?
- He knows what he was doing.
- It was a choice, not a mistake, because he has been with this woman for years.
- He could have given me “aids” or a “sti.”
- He gave me “aids/sti.”
- He started another family. My children and I weren’t enough for him!
- He is wicked, and I am not wasting my time.
- I will never forgive him after what he did.
- It’s not like he cheated, and I heard the girl is my best friend, neighbor, co-worker, sister, babysitter, or maid.
- I am not forgiving him after all the disrespect and disgrace that he brought on the children and me.
- I will not forgive him! After he cheated and left me and the kids to suffer.
- Man a dog, and a leper never change their spot.
- Once a cheater, always a cheater.

- I deserve better, and I don't owe him any obligation.
- I don't need to forgive him. He went outside the marriage, not me.
- God understands, and the Bible gives permission to divorce if caught in the act of adultery.
- I love and forgive my husband, but can never trust him again.

After moving into a new environment with my husband, I thought, *"Fresh start and a new beginning."* How convinced I was. Since he decided to come, and everything was now behind us, I forgave him. We are still together, indicating that I have truly forgiven him, but I won't forget. If I never forgave him, I would not have stayed.

Let us face it: we always try to justify ourselves and our actions. However, forgiveness is not just a mere saying; it should be reflected in our words, deeds, and actions if we truly forgive someone. Now that I was working, I started going out and interacting with others. The more I engaged in discussions surrounding relationships and marriage, the angrier I felt, especially when I attended functions and listened to other men speak about their wives and how they respected them and their marriage. Additionally, when I conversed with people who showed interest in me, and I shared my story, and they responded, it made it worse. I searched for answers and validation because I started to feel embarrassed and uncomfortable with my husband.

As time progressed, I found that my actions were saying something totally different. As any situation arises, I would bring up everything from the past as a caution. If he stayed out late, I thought He was with another woman, no matter how he tried to explain. I would become very anxious to call his phone and raise arguments. I felt more anger growing towards him and thought the only way out was to seek revenge. I intentionally sought ways to get back at him because I thought I would feel justified after that and truly forgive him. I became very disrespectful and rebelled. I refused to continue performing my duties as a wife, and I just didn't want to be around him anymore, especially after he kept staying out late, going to parties, and keeping his phone silent. I decided that if he did not change completely, then I would become the worst nightmare ever.

I exhausted myself, trying to get back at my husband, causing us to start quarreling again. We got to a point where we began to neglect each other, and all I wanted now was for us to separate. Our actions toward each other made us bitter, causing us to lose ourselves. However, no matter what happened, we were still together, and neither of us was going anywhere. God was there along the way in every way I sought to leave.

I tried crossing boundaries I never thought I would, but God would show up in ways that only left a conviction. Like David, *"If I ascend up into heaven, thou art there: If I make my bed in hell, behold, thou art there." (Psalm 139:8 - KJV).* During this time, I discovered I had a sinful nature that was waiting to surface. God was there in every moment and was with me in every valley I traversed, trying to escape the continuation of my marriage. I did not realize that God was only using the situation to help me build resilience.

One day, while having a discussion with a lady friend who was experiencing infidelity, she stated that the conviction came to her to forgive her husband. She noted that she had examined herself, and when she looked back on her life, she saw that she had made mistakes many times. She pointed out that, as women, we are very careful to protect ourselves and keep secrets. The conversation took us to a place of identifying that we lust, we flirt, and it doesn't make us any different as it relates to the Word of God. At this moment, I learned that before we come to Christ, we are all sinners. We are saved by grace, and Lamentations 3:22 states, *"It is of the LORD's mercies that we are not consumed, because his compassions fail not." (KJV).*

Take a few moments and reflect on the grace of God.

I have learned from the old school, *"Two wrongs don't make it right."* Also, God made it clear across the board: *"Ye have heard that it was said by them of old time, thou shalt not commit adultery: but I say unto you, that whosoever looketh on a woman to lust after her hath committed adultery with her already in his heart." (Matthew 5:27-28 - KJV).*

I dissect the scripture to highlight how God views sin by examining the heart to perfect us. The fact that we think about things means that if the opportunity presents itself, we can fall into the same temptation. The woman in the Bible who was caught in the act of adultery was brought to Jesus, and *"He lifted up himself, and said unto them, He that is without sin among you, let him first cast a stone at her." (John 8:7 - KJV).*

Jesus was not condoning sin, nor was He making an excuse; His response showed that we all have flaws and should extend forgiveness and mercy as we all need it in some way. Remembering the story of David and Bathsheba in 2 Samuel 11, her nakedness caused his sinful nature to surface, and he sinned against God. The story went further because David used his authority and caused the death of Uriah, Bathsheba's husband. However, today, we benefit greatly from David's experience and transformation after God forgives him.

Also, in the story of Samson and Delilah, after Samson realized what had happened to him, he prayed, and God extended mercy to Him. The Bible states that *"he killed many more when he died than while he lived."* And Samson said, "Let me die with the Philistines!" And he bowed himself with all his might; and the house fell upon the lords and upon all the people that were therein. So, the dead which he slew at his death were more than they which he slew in his life. (Judges 16:30 - KJV). It doesn't matter who we are, our flesh is likely to fail us sometimes. I am not trying to justify the act of our spouses; I am bringing us all to a place of understanding the nature of our flesh and coming to terms with the fact that we all need forgiveness. Also, to acknowledge that when some things surface through the action of an individual, it is a cry for help. Life is more spiritual than physical, and it is important to understand and see things from a physical and spiritual perspective to help us overcome and forgive by identifying the causes from both angles. These situations are not a surprise to God; He knows exactly what He is doing in your life through you in the life of your husband.

As mentioned, overcoming the pain of infidelity is a process. Unforgiveness is one of the enemy's greatest weapons. I noticed that the harder we are on ourselves, the harder we will be, especially to those who hurt us. But as mentioned, the moment I released myself from the prison of unforgiveness, I stopped throwing tantrums and realized I needed to forgive my husband and move forward. Unfortunately, many people believe that forgiveness means the person has gotten away with what they did, and they will never change. In fact, some people believe that forgiving will only make them vulnerable and that people will only take them for granted. Yes, I felt that way, too, and to add, as Christians, we feel as if we are the only ones who deserve to be forgiven.

Forgiving yourself and others will free you and allow you to walk in peace. Don't let pride get in the way of healing and pursuing forgiveness. This will only breed anger and selfishness, leading you to believe you deserve to be with someone better. Nothing is wrong; the feeling is natural, but the truth is, no matter what decision you make, whether to stay or leave the marriage, it is very important to choose forgiveness to avoid stagnation and continuation of error in the future.

I remember when the Lord convinced me to forgive my husband as if nothing had happened, to go forward in His peace, and to leave everything to Him. It was direct, but I knew He was about to do something. I decided to be obedient to the voice of God. In this season, things became hard; every thought and scene became a song in my head, and I allowed my mind to process questions: *How can I forgive someone who slept with the neighbor, put me out of the house with our two kids, had the whole community laughing and mocking me, and told me to my face that he was not leaving this girl?* It didn't sound easy, but let me share what made it easy. One day, the Lord had me reflecting and asked, *"What if you were the one in the position? Wouldn't you want forgiveness?"* While I processed, I felt rage, ready to defend myself, and thought everyone makes mistakes; if I did something wrong, I would not allow anyone to judge me. As it is written in Matthew 22:14 KJV, "For many are called, but few are chosen." Sis, if you are that chosen one, then you have to be obedient to God. Moses had to stand in the gap, Jesus, the Son of righteousness, had to, and many others that we read about in history. All that is required of you is submission, alignment, and seeking the help needed. After I vented and calmed down, I started to break and heard the still, small voice. *How many times have I forgiven you?* I reflected and began to cry because that day

I had a deep introspection into myself and my husband, and the only thing I saw was that we needed God's help, and that help depended on me.

I sought help, and that was when I started attending the "Label Free Wives Events." At one of those events, the coach asked, *"Who taught your husband?"* That question bothered me as I thought of my husband and his journey growing up as a boy. She went further, teaching about negative generational patterns and generational curses, and identifying what was happening within the bloodline. It was with these sessions that the process of forgiveness became easier, as I now conclude that life is more spiritual than physical. I thought about our children and the kind of parents I want them to have, because our choices affect them. Also, the other question that changed my perspective was: *What if my son grows up and has the same shortcomings?* God forbid! But the truth be told, as mothers, we are very protective of our children, and for me, I would not want anyone to torture my son for the rest of his life. Because most of our men were not taught to be husbands from a biblical perspective, and I am not making excuses. I am reflecting on what the scripture says in Deuteronomy 5:9, *"Thou shalt not bow down thyself unto them, nor serve them: for I the LORD thy God am a jealous God, visiting the iniquity of the fathers upon the children unto the third and fourth generation of them that hate me." (KJV).*

Whether you decide to stay or leave, forgive your spouse for what he did and extend God's love to him. If children are involved, just remember your destination, as parents must be pure for their benefit. I say this because even if you choose to move on in a different relationship, if you have not perfected the heart of forgiveness, you still have not yet perfected the heart of love.

Charity suffereth long, and is kind; charity envieth not; charity vaunteth not itself, is not puffed up, doth not behave itself unseemly, seeketh not her own, is not easily provoked, thinketh no evil; Rejoiceth not in iniquity, but rejoiceth in the truth; Beareth all things, believeth all things, hopeth all things, endureth all things. (1 Corinthians 13:4-7 – KJV).

We live in a culture that encourages us to forgive but not forget, in order to instill fear about how we move forward. So, we move forward with a tendency to protect ourselves by holding on to the memories of things that caused us pain. This causes many people to get stuck in repeating cycles in their lives and other relationships, as they keep going back and rewinding what happened when faced with similar circumstances, making assumptions and drawing conclusions before finding a solution. Before you know it, the same thing happens again. God could have rewound and returned to Genesis 1 when Adam sinned because God gave them everything they needed in the garden. Also, remember the children of Israel, Solomon, David, and the many other prophets who went on before us that He appointed and anointed, yet they sinned against Him. He could have used all His experiences with man and limited His love and access to His Kingdom. However, the more men sinned and became wicked, the more compassion He had, causing Him to give His Son for us: Jesus, the Holy One, who had no sin, had to go through all the agony He did just for us.

The Bible says in Hebrews 4:15, *"For we have not an high priest which cannot be touched with the feeling of our infirmities; but was in all points tempted like as we are, yet without sin." (KJV).* God's love is unfailing, and so must we be to others with understanding, knowing that we have all been given forgiveness we do not deserve many times.

"He will turn again, he will have compassion upon us; he will subdue our iniquities; and thou wilt cast all their sins into the depths of the sea." (Micah 7:19 – KJV).

In this verse, God not only forgives, but all He forgives He places into the depths of the sea. Imagine the depth of the Pacific Ocean at 35,814 feet below sea level; its bottom is called the Challenger Deep, the deepest point known on Earth. That's how God forgives us, only because of His mercy and love towards us.

How can we achieve genuine forgiveness of others?

There are many excuses not to forgive. However: *"There is no love without forgiveness, and there is no forgiveness without love." —Bryant H. McGill*

To reinforce this quote, the Word of God emphasizes forgiveness and its relation to love. Let us examine a few scriptures that show the power of love and how it walks hand in hand with forgiveness.

"For God so loved the world, that he gave his only begotten Son, that whosoever believeth in him should not perish, but have everlasting life." (John 3:16 - KJV).

"And above all things have fervent charity among yourselves: for charity shall cover the multitude of sins." (1 Peter 4:8 - KJV).

"And forgive us our debts, as we forgive our debtors." (Matthew 6:12 -KJV).

"Then said Jesus, Father, forgive them; for they know not what they do. And they parted his raiment, and cast lots." (Luke 23:34 - KJV).

Saying we forgive with a "but" isn't true forgiveness: forgiveness is a process that can only be achieved through God's unconditional love, with compassion and mercy. God's unconditional love is a system of advantage that guarantees that we become a full expression of His character. John 3:16 highlights God's profound and unconditional love for us, demonstrated by the sacrifice of His only Son, Jesus, who died for our sins to be forgiven. I passionately say that the heart of love and forgiveness will enable us to overcome, be free, and be at peace with ourselves, the past, and others. If we don't forgive others, then God won't forgive us. God asks us to forgive because He has freely forgiven and shown us mercy. He wants us to forgive and be free from the pain of the past by changing the posture of our hearts towards our husbands. It is not easy, as it requires continual, painful surrendering to God. But He is there, willing to help you through forgiveness. You must trust Him because He is not asking you to do anything He has not done for you. When you forgive, it shows that God's forgiveness has significantly impacted you.

Prayer

Heavenly Father, I humble myself before You. I messed up many times, hurt and offended others, but You still forgive me, love me, and show me mercy. Thank You for forgiving me, and I ask that You help me forgive my husband. Teach me to love him and how to show him mercy as You do. In Jesus' Name. Amen.

REWRITE THE SAME SCRIPTURES AS A DECLARATION AND PERSONALIZE THEM

"And be ye kind one to another, tenderhearted, forgiving one another, even as God for Christ's sake hath forgiven you."

(Ephesians 4:32 – KJV).

____

____

Chapter 5

Forgive The Other Woman

One of the most significant challenges is forgiving the "Other Woman," which they call in our language "The Matie." In the 90s one of our respected artists released a song called "Matie a Nuh Good Something" along with so many other songs. See below:

1. **"Matie a Nuh Good Something" by Beenie Man**

This song condemned the role of the *Matie* (the other woman), stressing that being a mistress is dishonorable and destructive. It reflected a cultural attitude in the 90s that openly criticized women who entered relationships with married men.

2. **"Modelling" by Beenie Man**

In this track, Beenie Man draws a comparison between wives and mistresses, praising wives for their dignity, while mocking mistresses as lacking worth. Its lyrics often fueled heated exchanges in dancehall sessions, where women used it to throw insults at rivals.

3. **"You a Di Wife" by Beenie Man & ARP**

This song elevated wives above mistresses, affirming their rightful place as "the chosen one." It was an anthem for many married women at the time, reinforcing cultural beliefs that the wife always holds the highest status, regardless of infidelity.

These are some songs that hit number one, and I can remember vividly, even though I was a teenager then, how they were used to provoke arguments and fights with women regularly, especially at parties, causing a build-up of hatred and anger towards women who were characterized as "The Matie." I was living in a shanty area then, and I witnessed many fights stemming from these songs, as women in relationships with the same person would pass by and sing, *"throwing words at each other."* Additionally, I had an experience close to home as my mom battled with "The Matie," who lived just a stone's throw away from where we resided. Here, we see a trend and a negative generational pattern.

As I stated in the earlier chapter, our culture has shaped our minds into believing that men cheat due to circumstances and issues that arise within their homes. They normalize this behavior as a means of comfort, while the guilt and blame rest on their wives. The understanding I get based on experience, culture, and religion is that women in these situations are to battle it out with themselves. The wives are expected to remain in their positions as the chosen ones, and the Matie usually remains for as long as the man pleases, no matter what.

As a church girl, I was told to trust God and pray because *"him soon change."* Scriptures were also thrown at me. Let's examine a few:

- *"And he saith unto them, Whosoever shall put away his wife, and marry another, committeth adultery against her. And if a woman shall put away her husband and be married to another, she committeth adultery." (Mark 10:11-12 – KJV).*

- *"And unto the married I command, yet not I, but the Lord, Let not the wife depart from her husband:" (1 Corinthians 7:10 - KJV).*

- *"He saith unto them, Moses because of the hardness of your hearts suffered you to put away your wives: but from the beginning it was not so. And I say unto you, Whosoever shall put away his wife, except it be for fornication, and shall marry another, committeth adultery: and whoso*

> *marrieth her which is put away doth commit adultery."* *(Matthew 19:8-9 - KJV).*

In these scriptures, we can see that divorce is prohibited for just about anything. However, in Matthew 19:8-9, Jesus clarified, with Moses, that it was because of the hardness of the heart that men divorce over simple matters, but He went ahead to state that divorce is permitted if one commits adultery. Marriage is not just a commitment but also a covenant, and when any individual gets involved sexually outside their marriage, the covenant is broken. This is why we experience so much warfare as women and see each other as the enemy. As I stated, life is more spiritual than physical, and when a covenant with God is broken, it is akin to backsliding, as if we are no longer under His protection and are now left open to contend.

Husband: *house-band - "hus" is the old spelling of "house" and "band" concerns his bond to the house that he owns*. This shows the importance of husbands and how their lifestyle affects everyone involved.

Culturally, when I engaged in conversation with persons who were not yet converted, they would say things like, *"A man all over; dem a dawg," "Like father like son," "Nuh care weh yuh do, dem a go cheat. As long as him a tek care a yuh and children, nuh pay him no mind,"* and it goes on. Some would go as far as to share how they grew up and saw their father cheating multiple times on their mother, but she still washed and played her role as a wife because he ensured the family was provided for, as they gave them time to change. Others stated that their mother loved their father and didn't want to leave because of the children. Some say, *"She is in her church and trusts God because it's the devil."* To conclude, with all that said, the belief is that the other woman is the main problem and is only trying to destroy their home and *"Dem nah leave dem husband fi nuh woman come take over."* Wow! The conviction is so firm as it relates to why men cheat, and the other women are seen as the problem.

In a discussion, most wives shared that they forgive their husbands but do not intend to drop their guard with the other woman/women. With long debates expressing that they did not owe "the other woman" any obligation because she is the one who slept with their husband, they expressed with anger, *"She knew he was married! They are homewreckers. I'm not so nice. Me nah laugh up wid no women weh tek my husband. Once bitten, twice shy. If she gets the chance again, she will sleep with him. Dem probably still hiding and doing it the same way."* Just imagine the tone and atmosphere of these discussions. I was at no time feeling offended when they blurted out at me, and neither did I second-guess forgiving the other woman, "the Mattie." It is important and a must-do if we really say we are forgiving ourselves and our husbands and moving forward in spite of our decision.

And he said unto them, When ye pray, say, Our Father which art in heaven, Hallowed be thy name. Thy kingdom come. Thy will be done, as in heaven, so in earth. Give us day by day our daily bread. And forgive us our sins; for we also forgive every one that is indebted to us. And lead us not into temptation; but deliver us from evil. (Luke 11:2-4 – KJV).

In July 2020, I had a vision that I was driving a high Jeep, and when I reached a certain place, a roadblock blocked my path to my destination. Based on the jeep's height in the dream, I could see my destination, but when I tried to get around, there was a blockage. When I looked to the left, I saw a light showing me a path, but because of the jeep's size, I could not get past it. At that time, I was in the process of getting a mortgage to purchase a property. I submitted all my documents, and the Loan officer, who was very kind, just changed his mind, handed everything back to me, and said it wasn't possible. That evening, when I got back the documents, I was disappointed. However, I was redirected to another loan officer for assistance, and he handled everything and processed the records, but something was holding up the process. I remember praying and asking my pastor to pray the Sunday at church.

The following Monday morning, on my way out to work, I was reminded of the vision and asked God to reveal its meaning to me. All I heard was the still, small voice saying clearly and precisely, *"You need to forgive…"* and He spoke the name of the person. I felt hot. I felt cold. I got uncomfortable. I pondered on it for the rest of the day through to Wednesday, and when I could not take the conviction anymore, I called both my pastor and his wife into a meeting. I explained all that was happening to them and asked for their input just to get relief. They were quiet for a moment, then my pastor's wife asked, *"How do you plan on doing this?"* Trembling and sweating, I said, *"Meet with her. Call her!"* I was all over the place, anxious. When she realized what was happening to me, she gave her feedback on the situation, and then my pastor said, *"Whatever the Lord tells you to do, do it."* Ah, I felt my whole life in seconds sink into disarray.

Following up on Saturday morning, I was outside sweeping when I felt a shadow over me, and I started to feel as if I was about to pass out. I dropped my broom, ran to my room, and fell on the bed. I heard clearly, *"Today you are going to call and tell her you forgive her."* I said, *"No, no. I'm not calling her. God, how can I forgive her when she knew we were married? She knew I just had two babies trying to raise. Forgive someone who boldly stepped up to me and told me to my face, 'She and my husband deh and dem naah lef?' Forgive someone who saw me walking with my children and called them names, after all that she was already putting me through? Forgive someone who lived right next door and decided that with all forces she was going to destroy me?"*

I can remember it like it was yesterday. While writing now, I am smiling because the presence of the Lord was over me, waiting for my obedience. The feeling got worse; I made excuses, saying that I didn't know the number and it had been years since I had last seen her. Now, by this time, I felt death over me quickly. I fell to the ground with my hands raised, and I said, *"Yes, Lord. I surrender."* I felt relief, and her number came back to my memory with much trembling. I took up the phone, dialed the number, and she answered. I was smiling when she answered. I greeted her and said, *"The Lord led me to call, and I just want to say I forgive you, and I'm sorry for anything I did or said in the past that offended you."* She replied, *"Thank you for calling. I have been waiting for this call. I saw you one day in the supermarket, and I wanted to approach, but I wasn't sure where you were after all the pain and trouble I had caused you, so I prayed for us, and here we are."* She apologized too. The rest is history because we spent the rest of the day talking and laughing over the past, and to this date, she is not just a friend but a sister whom I love dearly. We communicate like two sisters; it may not be on a regular basis, but we do, and when we see each other, we greet with a hug. You cannot tell whether she was the other woman just by looking at us. She and her daughter are the best thing that could ever happen in my life because it is this experience that has helped me to master the art of forgiveness and the love of God flowing through me.

Sister, it was an experience I will never forget. From then on, both our lives changed for the better.

The Monday morning after that weekend, I received an early call from the loan officer to come to the bank and sign some documents. I went, and it was for a company bus I had given up on. On Wednesday of that same week, I got the call to come again to sign, and here came the release for the property. We didn't have the deposit for the property, and God opened doors for us. God amazed me even more by allowing the property owners to give me the blueprint for the property, voiding the hassle. For almost one year, the applications were held, then released, in obedience to God and in forgiveness. The rest of my life, to this date and going forward, is history as God continues to make manifest His will and purpose for my life.

Forgiveness is freedom. You have wasted enough of your time fighting the wrong person; the "Matie" is not the enemy. Start fighting the real enemy: pay attention to the spirits operating and manipulating you, your husband, and the other woman. I take this opportunity to ask you to extend this to others you suspect have partaken in or are partaking in the act of infidelity within your marriage. The other woman could even be your sister or close friend; it's hard to see beyond them what you see in the physical, but get down to business and start fighting the real devil. Forgive her; it's a big deal and a new start for you both.

REWRITE THE SAME SCRIPTURES AS A DECLARATION AND PERSONALIZE THEM

"And forgive us our debts, as we forgive our debtors." (Matthew 6:12 – NKJV).

____

____

Chapter 6

Getting Past the Pain of Infidelity

Life happens as we journey through. The shock, betrayal, unexpected disappointments, pain, setbacks, and the ongoing heartache are an experience that leaves a scar, especially if a child or children are involved. However, these experiences can serve as a learning mechanism as we navigate our future to avoid struggles, stagnation, and things that weigh us down. In fact, getting past the pain of infidelity is freedom from bitterness, anger, anxiety, self-doubt, fear, and the roadblocks of unforgiveness. Forgiveness is the most challenging, so getting past this hurdle makes things easier.

Choosing to get past it has made me realize that life is more spiritual than physical, and if we were to pay attention to the people who caused us pain in the flesh, we would never be unstuck. In fact, this decision is not just for your benefit but for your spouse, your children, and, surprisingly, for many others, and generations to come after. This will leave a legacy of peace, understanding, and others, along with generations to come, will remember that you chose to let go and let God.

As you address the underlying issues, its benefits will positively impact the growth and development of a more substantial relationship, whether you choose to stay or separate. The willingness to work through things together is a mature decision. After all, upon deciding to get past the pain, I was shocked when I realized how much work I had to do personally, along with my husband, and the underlying issues within my marriage; it was very painful.

Praying and fasting are excellent; counseling is good; and being part of a community helps tremendously. Traveling only takes you away from the situation physically. It is when you finally come to terms with yourself to get past the pain that you will ultimately persevere. Just like Jesus in the Garden of Gethsemane, He decided to get past the pain and allow God's will to process itself, knowing that after this He would preside.

"Saying, Father, if thou be willing, remove this cup from me: nevertheless not my will, but thine, be done." (Luke 22:42 - KJV).

Jesus was overwhelmed and distressed with the suffering, but He let go to get past it. Choosing to let go and get past the pain will demand the flesh to die, and ultimately, the feelings of revenge and all other emotions mentioned throughout. At this point, I invite you to pause and allow God to take complete control and help you get past that lingering pain that wants to hinder you from restoring and inflicting guilt now that you have forgiven yourself, your spouse, the other woman, and others.

"Sometimes we have to be broken down so that we can be rebuilt into what we're actually meant to be." —Your Tango

As I navigated past the pain, I realised that the generational curses were domineering on both sides of our family. However, it posed a great opportunity for change because the fact is, the majority of us have been visited by the sins of our fathers.

"Thou shalt not bow down thyself unto them, nor serve them: for I the Lord thy God am a jealous God, visiting the iniquity of the fathers upon the children unto the third and fourth generation of them that hate me." (Deuteronomy 5:9 – KJV).

We are facing battles our fathers started, and no one seems to have taken the time to address them spiritually. So, I agree with the late Dr. Munroe, who stated that *"When situations arise and challenges come, God wants to reintroduce Himself to us differently."*

"The law of the LORD is perfect, converting the soul: The testimony of the LORD is sure, making wise the simple." (Psalm 19:7 – KJV).

I believe God allowed us to make our own marriage choices to work through us in the bloodline of our spouses for His Name's sake and our children. Just as the sins of our fathers visited us, I believe that our righteousness and connection with God will be a countertransference to our children just the same. As the Word of God declares in *Proverbs 14:34, "Righteousness exalteth a nation: but sin is a reproach to any people." (KJV).* God was with me as He promised in Psalm 23, and so is He with you in this time, and even as you read and meditate on what is shared.

Another victory in overcoming the pain is that you will learn how to walk closer with God and participate in His program designed to break generational curses. Throughout my years, I can attest that I found myself in a situation I never thought I would be in. To add, I discovered that my husband and I had adopted many of the negative generational patterns that needed God's intervention. No one taught us how to be a wife or husband according to the Word of God, nor did we grow up in a home with parents who demonstrated the roles and responsibilities of a wife and a husband and what a real family is about. Out of eight siblings, my husband was the first to get married; his parents and my parents lived together for years before marriage. So, taking such a bold step was a plus, and I began to understand why we had to fight so many battles.

The pain of infidelity is not an easy walk over, especially after years of investing yourself in the marriage. It requires a lot of ongoing work, and there will be days when your mind and emotions will make you feel stupid and hopeless, and that is okay; give yourself grace, it is sufficient. Also, Isaiah 59:19 says "So shall they fear the name of the Lord from the west, and his glory from the rising of the sun. When the enemy shall come in like a flood, the Spirit of the Lord shall lift up a standard against him."

However, it is unhealthy to dwell on what happened and blame yourself, thinking it could have been avoided. You must choose to get unstuck and keep moving past the dormancies in your life.

Getting past the pain is a resurrection from where you are to where God wants you to be. After pain and suffering, how we appear is very important; our children, especially, are watching. I can attest, and you can too, because some of us still talk about what our parents did and what they didn't do, and we blame them. However, take notice that after Jesus was raised from the dead, the first persons He appeared to were His disciples, reassuring them and then instructing them to go and spread the good news. He ensured they had evidence to build their confidence to stop mourning Him and go forth. Now, the disciples could speak boldly because Jesus had fulfilled His promise. It is the same with us; our children depend on us when we smile and tell them everything will be okay. We must give them evidence and confidence to trust us. Also, in Revelation 1:18, Jesus stood boldly and declared, *"I am he that liveth, and was dead; and, behold, I am alive for evermore, Amen; and have the keys of hell and of death." (KJV).* Wow! What a victory after letting go of His will and allowing the suffering to process Him.

I encourage you just the same to push past the pain and govern the hell that the enemy has broken out into your family and avoid death. Especially if you decide to work things out with your spouse, and even if you choose not to stay in the marriage, it is still vital.

In 1 Samuel 1:1, the Bible gives us a perfect example of what the pain of infidelity causes us when we realise that it really happened, especially if a child is involved. In those days, the law permitted a man to have more than one wife, especially if his first wife was barren. It was lawful for a man to get children with another woman to carry on his name. It was a big deal, and a woman was scorned and seen as unworthy for not bearing a child. In this chapter, the story tells us of a man named Elkanah who had two wives: Hannah and Penninah. It stated that Penninah had children, but that Hannah had none. Elkanah loved Hannah, but the Lord had shut up her womb. And because of this, her adversary Penninah "the other woman" provoked her to make her fret, because the Lord had shut up her womb. Just imagine the pain that Hannah was feeling and the weight of the pain that she was carrying to the point where she hardly ate and grieved a lot. Further along in the story, it made us aware of other effects it had on Hannah; it stated that she was bitter within her soul (that is deep). We can relate to that!

However, Hannah decided to get past the pain. The Bible says that Hannah rose up after she had eaten and drunk, which means that Hannah had now made a decision. She went up into the temple and prayed unto the Lord and vowed a vow: Victory. See the passage below:

Now there was a confident man of Ramathaimzophim, of mount Ephraim, and his name was Elkanah, the son of Jeroham, the son of Elihu, the son of Tohu, the son of Zuph, an Ephrathite: And he had two wives; the name of the one was Hannah, and the name of the other Peninnah: and Peninnah had children, but Hannah had no children. And this man went up out of his city yearly to worship and to sacrifice unto the LORD *of hosts in Shiloh. And the two sons of Eli, Hophni and Phinehas, the priests of the* LORD, *were there. And when the time was that Elkanah offered, he gave to Peninnah his wife, and to all her sons and her daughters, portions: But unto Hannah he gave a worthy portion; for he loved Hannah: but the* LORD *had shut up her womb. And her adversary also provoked her sore, for to make her fret, because the* LORD *had shut up her womb. And as he did so year by year, when she went up to the house of the* LORD, *so she provoked her; therefore she wept, and did not eat. Then said Elkanah her husband to her, Hannah, why weepest thou? and why eatest thou not? and why is thy heart grieved? am not I better to thee than ten sons? So Hannah rose up after they had eaten in Shiloh, and after they had drunk. Now Eli the priest sat upon a seat by a post of the temple of the* LORD. *And she was in bitterness of soul, and prayed unto the LORD, and wept sore. And she vowed a vow, and said, O LORD of hosts, if thou wilt indeed look on the affliction of thine handmaid, and remember me, and not forget thine handmaid, but wilt give unto thine handmaid a man child, then I will give him unto the LORD all the days of his life, and there shall no razor come upon his head. And it came to pass, as she continued praying before the LORD, that Eli marked her mouth. Now Hannah, she spake in her heart; only her lips moved, but her voice was not heard: therefore Eli thought she had been drunken. And Eli said unto her, How long wilt thou be drunken? put away thy wine from thee. And Hannah answered and said, No, my lord, I am a woman of a sorrowful spirit: I have drunk neither wine nor strong drink, but have poured out my soul before the LORD. Count not thine handmaid for a daughter of Belial: for out of the abundance of my complaint and grief have I spoken hitherto. Then Eli answered and said, Go in peace: and the God of Israel grant thee thy petition that thou hast asked of him. And she said, Let thine handmaid find grace in thy sight. So the woman went her way, and did eat, and her countenance was no more sad. (1 Samuel 1:1-18 - KJV).*

When a child is involved, it feels like the pain has become a part of you, and if you choose to stay with your husband, it would feel as if the pain will forever be a part of you. But notice what Hannah did after her husband asked her those thought-provoking questions. She became aware and arose and went and prayed unto the Lord, pouring out her heart to Him quietly, and made a vow unto Him. Hannah knew the power of humility, silence, and prayer.

The pain is temporary; only for a season and a reason, as in Ecclesiastes 3. The pain is not to kill us but to teach us that there are things within our lives that God wants to teach us how to navigate and get past them. God wants to teach you strategies, give you a new mindset, and teach you how to "*be ye kind one to another, tenderhearted, forgiving one another, even as God for Christ's sake hath forgiven you." (Ephesians 4:32 - KJV).*

Learn the difference between others and even yourself. Infidelity is a pandemic, and we can relate to the COVID-19 pandemic of 2019 and how it affected the world. However, despite its adverse effects, there were some positive effects. To name a few: it helped build genuine relationships, usher in new tools and software, encourage lifestyle changes to practice better hygiene, drive innovation, and more. A perfect example is that you are still alive, which means you survived and learned to navigate and overcome the negatives and hurdles of the COVID-19 pandemic.

You are a winner, and you can get past. Unfortunately, many of us, especially Christians, have been struggling with truly getting past the pain of infidelity because of shame and reproach. So many women find themselves still hesitant and anxious, only because of expectations. Yes, for real! You are expected to forgive quickly and move forward. Getting past the pain, as I said, is not easy, but it is possible. Set boundaries and goals, and every day, choose to embrace and take one step forward past the pain. Life happens, and it is a journey. On this journey called life, we will encounter heartbreak, disappointment, failures, and sometimes loss. But it is not to destroy you; your pain is your purpose. So, manipulate your pain for a purpose.

Apostle Paul encourages us to put the things of the past behind us and focus on the journey before us with determination.

REWRITE THE SAME SCRIPTURES AS A DECLARATION AND PERSONALIZE THEM

Brethren, I count not myself to have apprehended: but this one thing I do, forgetting those things which are behind, and reaching forth unto those things which are before. I press toward the mark for the prize of the high calling of God in Christ Jesus.

(Philippians 3:13-14 – KJV).

____

____

____

____

____

Be aware of the situation!

- Make a decision.
- Pray. Pray. Pray.

- Humble yourself before God.
- Know your purpose.
- Think of the long-term effects.
- Trust God.

Chapter 7

Be The Victor and Not the Victim

The dictionary defines a victim as one who has been harmed, injured, or killed as a result of a crime, accident, or other event or action. A victim is "present continuous" and deemed as a sufferer, expecting to suffer as if there is no ending. Hence, a victor is the winner, overcomer, and defeater of all adversaries.

Earlier, I mentioned the belief and shared the views on men who cheat from a religious and cultural aspect. One popular saying is "man a dawg" or "a leopard never changes its spot." This belief and terminology is not just a saying but also a negative behavioural pattern seen within most men's actions to this date. I will not go in depth, but after going through the process of forgiving and with every effort to get past the pain, another woman appeared, saying she was pregnant with a child for my husband. However, it was at this moment that I realised God was placing a demand on me. I was shaken, but for some reason God gave me the strength to deal with the situation with such wisdom that brought about a positive turnaround in my life, leaving me in awe to this day. I smile as the victor because I now understand what God is doing. I just don't know the rest of the process. I reflected on the story of Joseph, who was thrown into a pit by his brothers out of envy because he was his father, Jacob's, favorite, and because of his dream to become great (see Genesis 37).

Life comes with many challenges, but we must be careful not to let them turn us into victims. At first, I took it very personally and was angry, despite how God had inspired me to navigate this season. However, I was very conscious this time in everything and every season and paid close attention to all the repetitions in the situation.

Firstly, I realised that this wave of infidelity came stronger; the difference is that the other woman was very humble. Secondly, it was trying to pull me back to where I was, how I felt, and how I reacted with the first wave. We must learn to adjust ourselves in the different areas of our lives after specific experiences. As I mentioned earlier about COVID-19, if we go back, we would realise that when it first hit, many of the measures in place now were not yet in place. However, over time, all the necessary adjustments were gradually made and changes implemented so that life could go on. The government, along with all the other members of parliament and the sector, had to come to an agreement and enforce rules to restart and accommodate everyone's operations. This did not happen overnight; careful planning and thought went into it before any actions could be taken. Schools and churches went online, and we had to social distance, with only a few allowed in a space. It was chaos in the hospitals, and people were just dying, causing many to panic and become overwhelmed. It was so calm and quiet. Despite all that was happening, I could sense a peace, especially with the absence of loud music. Everyone was on alert and became very cautious. When the second wave came, the response was much better because the government had reviewed its weaknesses, adjusted accordingly, and prepared better.

Why was all this done? To control the spread of the disease that was causing many victims. Why did we obey and stay on alert? Because we didn't want to become victims, we scorned each other. After going through the healing process by forgiving and getting past the pain, I started to build my walls of trust and confidence again; however, I had to decide that, come what may, I would not be the victim; I would become the victor.

How do we become the victor in a situation like this? A victor defies all odds, despite all the significant obstacles, and succeeds in all things—through God—that seemed impossible. The most significant is mastering the heart of forgiveness and offering to those who caused you pain the unconditional love of God.

"For God so loved the world, that he gave his only begotten Son, that whosoever believeth in him should not perish, but have everlasting life." (John 3:16 – KJV).

We all know the story of the death and resurrection of Jesus, the Son of God, who is our victor today, and we now live a victorious life through Him. He achieved victory by overcoming all the obstacles that faced mankind.

"Surely he took up our pain and bore our suffering, yet we considered him punished by God, stricken by him, and afflicted. But he was pierced for our transgressions, he was crushed for our iniquities; the punishment that brought us peace was on him, and by his wounds we are healed. We all, like sheep, have gone astray, each of us has turned to our own way; and the Lord has laid on him the iniquity of us all. He was oppressed and afflicted, yet he did not open his mouth; he was led like a lamb to the slaughter, and as a sheep before its shearers is silent, so he did not open his mouth. By oppression and judgment he was taken away. Yet who of his generation protested? For he was cut off from the land of the living; for the transgression of my people he was punished. He was assigned a grave with the wicked, and with the rich in his death, though he had done no violence, nor was any deceit in his mouth. Yet it was the Lord's will to crush him and cause him to suffer, and though the Lord makes his life an offering for sin, he will see his offspring and prolong his days, and the will of the Lord will prosper in his hand. After he has suffered, he will see the light of life and be satisfied; by his knowledge my righteous servant will justify many, and he will bear their iniquities. Therefore I will give him a portion among the great, and he will divide the spoils with the strong,

because he poured out his life unto death, and was numbered with the transgressors. For he bore the sin of many, and made intercession for the transgressors." (Isaiah 53:4-12 – NIV).

We saw earlier in Revelation how He rose victoriously, walked straight into hell, and took back the keys of hell and of death.

Walk, talk, and live like a victor, and take back that which God promises you by faith through the choices you make and the way you react. A victor seeks to discover purpose, that is, *"What God tells you to do,"* will allow you to navigate confidently, effectively, and victoriously. A victor must ensure that all past experiences are properly processed by overcoming and seeking success in the areas of their life that challenge them most. As stated, a victor is the winner, overcomer, and defeater of all adversaries. You must decide you are going to win with yourself and not try to win against the other woman or your husband. A victor is bold and courageous as commanded in Joshua 1:9, *"Have not I commanded thee? Be strong and of a good courage; be not afraid, neither be thou dismayed: for the LORD thy God is with thee whithersoever thou goest." (KJV).*

A victor is one who, after their experience and with all that they have learned, can look now in the face of adversaries, be victorious, and seek opportunities to glorify God in future situations.

"The Spirit of the Lord GOD is upon me; because the LORD hath anointed me to preach good tidings unto the meek; he hath sent me to bind up the brokenhearted, to proclaim liberty to the captives, and the opening of the prison to them that are bound; to proclaim the acceptable year of the LORD, and the day of vengeance of our God; to comfort all that mourn; to appoint unto them that mourn in Zion, to give unto them beauty for ashes, the oil of joy for mourning, the garment of praise for the spirit of heaviness; that they might be called trees of righteousness, the planting of the LORD, that he might be glorified." (Isaiah 61:1-3 – KJV).

A victor depends on the anointing God has placed on their lives to overcome the most drastic experiences in their lives to help others, to tell them of the good news of how they overcome, to bring comfort, healing, hope, and to set those in the captivity of infidelity free. I have seen too many women over the years fighting, quarreling, comparing themselves, underestimating each other, competing, and becoming enemies. In the end, the results are never pleasant for either.

So, are you going to remain a victim, or will you become the victor?

Refuse to fail, go under, and allow God to turn your mess into a message. We have witnessed many victims of infidelity to date because they refuse to forgive, get past the pain, and face their fear.

I agree with this quote by picturequotes.com: *"Great is the victory that is gained without bloodshed."*

This quote is very deep, and I believe that your reading this book shows that you are a victor because a true victor is one who uses their ability to resolve conflicts, rise above them, and go forth living a purposeful life without destroying or harming anyone. Become so authentic as a victor that no one will be able to tell your story, unless you share your journey with them.

When I share my testimony, people would be in awe—to God be the glory—because they see the reflection of a victor when they look at me, especially for those who know and were part of the experience of my story. They can testify that my relationship with my husband to date does not reflect how he once treated me, because I have allowed God to perfect that which concerns me and to teach me how to be a victor in the midst of adversity, while still loving and caring for those who are causing me pain. The pain is only temporary and for a season, because after all is done, when we arise to be the victor, then everything will change eventually for good.

A victor does not try to overcome evil with evil, but do good as the Word of God commands in Matthew 5:44-48, *"But I say unto you, Love your enemies, bless them that curse you, do good to them that hate you, and pray for them which despitefully use you, and persecute you; that ye may be the children of your Father which is in heaven: for he maketh his sun to rise on the evil and on the good, and sendeth rain on the just and on the unjust. For if ye love them which love you, what reward have ye? do not even the publicans the same? And if ye salute your brethren only, what do ye more than others? do not even the publicans so? Be ye therefore perfect, even as your Father which is in heaven is perfect." (KJV).*

Proclaim Victory and be the Victor

I implore you to allow God to make you the victor today.

Share your concerns with God and talk to Him honestly about what's on your mind and heart.

Prayer

Heavenly Father, draw me close to You and teach me how to be the victor and not the victim. You are my strength. Teach my hands to war, and my fingers to fight the good fight of faith like You did with Elisha. In Jesus Name. Amen.

REWRITE THE SAME SCRIPTURES AS A DECLARATION AND PERSONALIZE THEM

"There is therefore now no condemnation to them which are in Christ Jesus, who walk not after the flesh, but after the Spirit."

(Romans 8:1 – KJV).

____

____

____

____

Chapter 8

Restore to Love Again

To learn how to love, we must begin with the source. God is love, and to know love (the agape) is to know God (become knowledgeable) and to live in love because to live is to love.

"Beloved, let us [unselfishly] love and seek the best for one another, for love is from God; and everyone who loves [others] is born of God and knows God [through personal experience]." (1 John 4:7 – AMP).

God's love is one of the greatest gifts given to mankind, and the core of everything God does stems from His love for us all. Expressively, throughout the Word of God, from Genesis to Revelation, its dominant theme is love.

To love again, you will need a made-up mind and the willingness to sacrifice to start the process and live a purposeful life. Here are some examples:

- *"For God so loved the world, that he gave his only begotten Son, that whosoever believeth in him should not perish, but have everlasting life." (John 3:16 – KJV).*

- *"But God commendeth his love toward us, in that, while we were yet sinners, Christ died for us."* (*Romans 5:8 - KJV).*

- *"But God, who is rich in mercy, for his great love where he loved us, even when we were dead in sins, hath quickened us together with Christ, (by grace ye are saved;)" (Ephesians 2:4-5 – KJV).*

To restore means to re-establish, put or bring back into existence or use. After this pandemic of infidelity, it is vital to re-establish your true purpose and learn to love God and yourself before you can love anyone else. When a loving relationship with God is established, love for ourselves and our neighbors becomes possible because sin broke the needed linkage in our ability to give and receive love. It is then crucial that we take time and allow the Spirit of God to help us understand how to let the love of God flow through us to others.

Outside of the love of God in us, you will not be able to restore and unconditionally go forward, loving your husband, ex-husband, the other woman, and other persons who tend to contribute to the great cause of this pandemic that you experience. We all need love and have fallen short at some point in loving, even our very spouse, unconditionally, before we understood the love of God.

In an earlier chapter, I reminded us of how the pandemic affected all of us, causing a lot of panic due to a lack of preparation and understanding. With this new experience, everyone, even our babies, had to learn new ways to survive and make many changes to accommodate and maintain our lives. It is the same as we navigate and return to love again. There are some things we must leave behind us, and one of them is blaming and a reminder of what happened in the past, causing us pain.

"He will turn again, he will have compassion upon us; he will subdue our iniquities; and thou wilt cast all their sins into the depths of the sea." (Micah 7:19 – KJV).

As you take the first step toward restoration, spend time developing healthy self-love. If God loves and has accepted you, then you should love and accept yourself. Do not be an enemy to yourself, because one of the biggest barriers within marriages that continues to cause a significant setback is self-love and acceptance. Everyone who feels incomplete and fails to love themselves tends to fail miserably in the other areas of their lives and relationships. This adds to a person significantly when they are faced with infidelity; they develop more self-hatred and become resentful of themselves because of the feelings of betrayal and unworthiness. Unfortunately, this has caused many women, after experiencing infidelity, to shy away and refuse to give themselves entirely within the same marriage or even when they move forward in other relationships. The trust is put out the door, confidence and the joy of just being married become numb. The willingness to live and to make sacrifices for a better future is aborted mentally, all because of the refusal to love yourself.

God has accepted us, even before we are born, with all our imperfections. Why restore us to love? I have forgiven, and is it even necessary? Yes, because love is a beautiful thing, and this started from the beginning. God first created everything that man needed, and then He created man, expressing love through His actions. Within the pandemic of infidelity, you lost hope, and if you have no hope, then there is no love. To continue in a healthy marriage, you must be willing to make sacrifices and offer agape love to your spouse. Even if you don't want to stay, it is still a necessity.

"Charity suffereth long, and is kind; charity envieth not; charity vaunteth not itself, is not puffed up, doth not behave itself unseemly, seeketh not her own, is not easily provoked, thinketh no evil; rejoiceth not in iniquity, but rejoiceth in the truth; beareth all things, believeth all things, hopeth all things, endureth all things." (1 Corinthians 13:4-7 - KJV).

"And above all things have fervent charity among yourselves: for charity shall cover the multitude of sins." (1 Peter 4:8 - KJV).

When you restore to love again, it is a sign of completeness and shows that you know your value and understand the importance of love, not just for yourself but also for others. If you have decided to break negative cycles within your life and your children's lives, then restoration is a must.

When infidelity steps in, the reality is that the radiance of your love changes, maybe gradually or efficiently; either way, it does. So, whatever we understand love to be when we meet our spouse, all that is gone, eventually leaving the marriage more like a commitment to finish what was started, despite the line drawn. After a while, as I shared earlier, I didn't want to see my husband, nor did I want to be seen with him, and I had no appetite for him. It made me irritable, and that was when I went deeper into myself and with God to help me. I remember praying about the situation and asking God for His intervention. I prayed and begged God to free me, and told God I wanted to divorce, and I wrestled. Afterwards, I found myself in deep meditation, and some questions were posed. I knew this was God because it was that still, small voice. I remembered the many times I had the upper hand to leave, but I did not, and that was when I went on the journey of restoring to love again.

I mentioned another case of infidelity. Yes, this tore down every wall I had started rebuilding in moving forward. I will discuss that in volume two, which will follow this book. What was there to restore after all? The love of God is destined to change my life, his life, my children, the other woman, others around me, and you reading this book. At this point, I was not the one fading; the father of my children started to fade, and it was so evident in his appearance. The guilt of all that happened began to eat him up, and it began to affect my children, our business, and our loved ones. As stated in the Word of God, "love covers a multitude of sin" (see 1 Peter 4:8).

God led me on a path of learning to love myself and love Him, so that I could, in turn, extend His love to the father of my children. This changed our entire life to this date. I started watching Dr. Munroe's teachings on self-love, marriage, and many other topics, which helped me develop my knowledge, understanding, and wisdom. As he referenced the Word of God, I took the time to read and allow the Word to preside over my life. The second I started doing this, everything about me began to change. I began to see my husband through the eyes of God.

God spoke to me, starting with questions, *"What if you were in his position, wouldn't you want mercy and someone who knows better to help you to do better? What kind of father do you want your children to have? Can't I choose you and use you as a point of contact on this earth to affect the father of your children so that they have a better future? I have been very patient with you in many circumstances, so can't I be patient with him? What if it were your brother? What would you want for him? What about your son? Wouldn't you want mercy for him?"* The many questions God posed caused me to take the time to be fully restored to His true agape love and to get on with life as if nothing had happened. To date, this has caused happiness for my children, and the love and respect I get from them, their dad, and others is amazing. God can restore you to His true agape love that will cause you to look beyond your spouse's faults, whether you choose to stay or not. God's love is not just for some but for all.

The late Dr. Munroe stated, *"Love that looks for a reason is love with conditions attached, and conditions give rise to expectations. Expectations inevitably lead to disappointments; disappointments lead to arguments, which strains the relationship and endangers fellowship."* Love within a marriage is to be like the love that Jesus has for His church: *"Husbands, love your wives, even as Christ also loved the church, and gave himself for it; that he might sanctify and cleanse it with the washing of water by the word, that he might present it to himself a glorious church, not having spot, or wrinkle, or any such thing; but that it should be holy and without blemish." (Ephesians 5:25-27 – KJV).*

Many of us have been expressing love towards each other based on tradition, culture, and what we see our parents and others do. However, love for each other must derive from and germinate in the Word of God, and from God in us, working together to make decisions in the family that articulate God's expectations for ourselves and our children.

If you are in a position and your husband is willing to learn and change, then be the one who is used by God to be effective in his life. Stop looking from a cultural perspective wherein some women will state that *"Dem naah build no man fi no other woman."* I was ignorant at one time and would have said the same, but I answered the questions I stated in this chapter and allowed God to use me humbly as a mouthpiece in my husband's life. I say, *"Whether we stay together, there is one thing we can't separate from doing with each other, and that is parenting."* So, for the children's sake, let us stop using cultural norms and stick it out without destructive behaviours and attitudes towards each other. Adopt the unconditional love of God and allow it to flow through you.

REWRITE THE SAME SCRIPTURES AS A DECLARATION AND PERSONALIZE THEM.

"Charity suffereth long, and is kind; charity envieth not; charity vaunteth not itself, is not puffed up, doth not behave itself unseemly, seeketh not her own, is not easily provoked, thinketh no evil; rejoiceth not in iniquity, but rejoiceth in the truth; beareth all things, believeth all things, hopeth all things, endureth all things." (1 Corinthians 13:4-7 - KJV).

____

____

Dear Reader,

I trust that you have read and understand what we go through; however, let us not take it personally. Instead, see yourself as the one who God has chosen to bring an end to the sufferings that stemmed from our fathers, and mothers, great, great, grandfathers and mothers who perished in battle because of a lack of knowledge.

"My people are destroyed for lack of knowledge: because thou hast rejected knowledge, I will also reject thee, that thou shalt be no priest to me: seeing thou hast forgotten the law of thy God, I will also forget thy children." (Hosea 4:6 – KJV).

We have been given access to materials that break down the biblical principles of truly forgiving others, along with books like the one you just read, written to help you. Sharing our experiences takes a lot of courage and boldness, but it is for the glory of God. Many of our sisters died sadly, defeated in battle, and waiting for the day of judgment. So, I am imploring you to commit yourself to God, submit completely to Him, and allow Him to do what no man can do for you (see Matthew 19:26).

You have read my story and seen His glory. Allow God to fix you and, through you, deliver others.

With love, your sister,
Camille Fender

Make this declaration: *"I will trust in the LORD with all my heart, and lean not to my own understanding. In all my ways, I will acknowledge Him, and He will direct my paths." (see Proverbs 3:5-6).*

Let's get started with this exercise.

I am excited!

Forgiving others is not a weakness, my sister, nor have you lost the battle. Yes, I know it hurts, and we have strong reasons not to because, yes, he broke the covenant selfishly, and she boldly wanted to prove a point, but get over it. Forgiving them is actually you deciding to win honestly and be free.

Forgiveness is very beneficial to your prosperity, living a quality life overall, and most of all, keeps you connected to God. It will indeed improve your mental, physical, and emotional health and rid you of all those unexplained headaches and pain.

"Be not wise in thine own eyes: Fear the LORD, and depart from evil." (Proverbs 3:7 - KJV).

Journal

Who are the people you need to forgive? List them:

What are the reasons why you do not want to release this offense?

____

____

____

____

____

____

____

____

____

How will choosing to forgive change your life?

____

____

____

____

____

____

____

____

____

____

____

What does the Bible say about forgiveness? Just share, do not Google.

In light of how God has forgiven you, shouldn't you also forgive those you are withholding forgiveness from? Spend time with God, ask Him to search your heart, and give Him any hurt that you carry.

How is it affecting you negatively? Be still and allow the Holy Spirit to minister to your heart, then write what He reveals to you.

What could forgiveness unlock in your life? Pray and ask God to reveal every hindrance and opportunity that has been blocked due to unforgiveness.

What is God inviting you to release? Ask Him (see Isaiah 1:18).

____

____

____

____

____

____

____

____

Now move forward:

"I press toward the mark for the prize of the high calling of God in Christ Jesus." (Philippians 3:14 – KJV).

Let's Pray

Heavenly Father, Abba, my helper, healer, deliverer, the I Am. I humble myself before You. As it is written, *"If my people, which are called by my name, shall humble themselves, and pray, and seek my face, and turn from their wicked ways; then will I hear from heaven, and will forgive their sin, and will heal their land."* Lord, in obedience, I submit to Your will, and I declare and decree that I will press toward the goal for the prize of the upward call of God in Christ Jesus.

Day 1

Be honest with God. Tell Him exactly how you feel; just pour it all out and invite Him in the process. He cares.

"Behold, I stand at the door, and knock: if any man hear my voice, and open the door, I will come in to him, and will sup with him, and he with me." (Revelation 3:20 - KJV).

"For we have not an high priest which cannot be touched with the feeling of our infirmities; but was in all points tempted like as we are, yet without sin." (Hebrews 4:15 - KJV).

And a woman having an issue of blood twelve years, which had spent all her living upon physicians, neither could be healed of any," (Luke 8:43 – KJV).

Listen to "Withholding Nothing" by William McDowell.

Day 2

Have faith in the process. Do not allow your feelings to overcome you. Instead, surrender your feelings and all the people to God.

"And forgive us our debts, as we forgive our debtors." (Matthew 6:12 – KJV).

"And be ye kind one to another, tenderhearted, forgiving one another, even as God for Christ's sake hath forgiven you." *(Ephesians 4:32 – KJV).*

"Blessed are the merciful: for they shall obtain mercy." (Matthew 5:7 – KJV).

Listen to "Break Every Chain" by Tasha Cobbs Leonard.

Day 3

Pray for these people. Pray for God's blessings, healing, deliverance, and for saving their souls. Prayer changes things, breaks chains, turns hearts of stone to flesh, and ushers healing. They need God's help.

"Confess your faults one to another, and pray one for another, that ye may be healed. The effectual fervent prayer of a righteous man availeth much." (James 5:16 – KJV).

Listen to "House of Prayer" by Eddie James.

Day 4

Create healthy boundaries. Choose what to think. Let your conversations be seasoned with grace about these people, or at the mention of their names. See them as God does.

"For God so loved the world, that he gave his only begotten Son, that whosoever believeth in him should not perish, but have everlasting life." (John 3:16 – KJV).

"Finally, brethren, whatsoever things are true, whatsoever things are honest, whatsoever things are just, whatsoever things are pure, whatsoever things are lovely, whatsoever things are of good report; if there be any virtue, and if there be any praise, think on these things." (Philippians 4:8 – KJV).

Listen to "Your Spirit" by Tasha Cobbs Leonard.

Day 5

Embrace the healing process gracefully. It will not happen immediately, so give yourself "grace" and "space."

"For by grace are ye saved through faith; and that not of yourselves: it is the gift of God: not of works, lest any man should boast." (Ephesians 2:8-9 - KJV).

Listen to "Gracefully Broken" by Tasha Cobbs Leonard.

Day 6

Wrestle with your angel. God gave them charge over you. He is with you in the valley. Continue in worship; the devil will come.

"And Jacob was left alone; and there wrestled a man with him until the breaking of the day. And when he saw that he prevailed not against him, he touched the hollow of his thigh; and the hollow of Jacob's thigh was out of joint, as he wrestled with him. And he said, Let me go, for the day breaketh. And he said, I will not let thee go, except thou bless me." (Genesis 32:24-26 – KJV).

"For he shall give his angels charge over thee, to keep thee in all thy ways." (Psalm 91:11 – KJV).

"Yea, though I walk through the valley of the shadow of death, I will fear no evil: for thou art with me; thy rod and thy staff they comfort me." (Psalm 23:4 – KJV).

Listen to "To Worship You I Live" by Israel & New Breed and "The Heart of Worship" by Michael W. Smith.

Day 7

Reflect on God's love for you and why He saved you.

"For God so loved the world, that he gave his only begotten Son, that whosoever believeth in him should not perish, but have everlasting life." (John 3:16 – KJV).

"He restoreth my soul: He leadeth me in the paths of righteousness for his name's sake." (Psalm 23:3 – KJV).

Listen to "God Made You Special" by Deniece Williams.

Prayer of Healing

Heavenly Father, I confess my faults to You. Forgive me for holding myself in the prison of unforgiveness, shame, hatred, bitterness, and anger. I recommit to You, give You my will, and ask for Your will for my life, in Jesus' name. Amen.

Write a letter of healing to yourself.

Forgiving Self Contractual Agreement

This contract is an agreement you will make as your accountability.

I ________________________________ sign this contract as an agreement and commitment to forgive myself, put the past behind me, and, with every effort, go forward in God's strength and "Overcome the Pain of Infidelity." I therefore commit myself on this date _____________ to continue with this process of forgiveness to others as long as I live, for the glory of God,

Signature

____

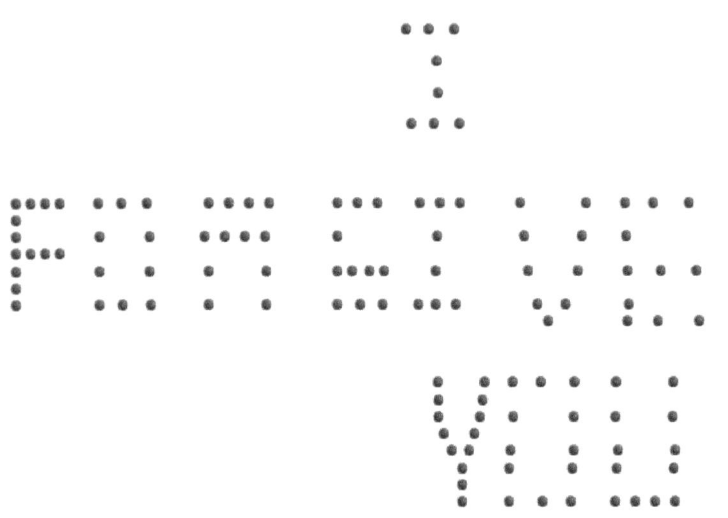

Listen to "Free" by Kirk Franklin

What is God saying to you?

About the Author

Camille Fender is a proud graduate of The Mico University College in Kingston, St. Andrew, Jamaica, where she earned her Master's degree in Guidance and Counseling. She is also an entrepreneur, certified Christian coach, ordained minister, wife, and mother.

Camille is passionate about motivating women to "Rise Above and Take a Stand," walking boldly in alignment with God's will and purpose for their lives. Her vision is to see women healed, restored, and empowered to embrace their true identity beyond pain and shame.

Her passion for helping women comes from her own story. Camille has endured the pain of infidelity and faced emotional, verbal, physical, and sexual abuse, along with seasons of neglect. Yet, through God's grace, she found strength to rise above every obstacle, choosing faith over fear, and purpose over pain. Her testimony is one of resilience, forgiveness, and victory in Christ.

Grounded in the biblical truth of Philippians 4:13, *"I can do all things through Christ who strengthens me,"* Camille lives to empower others with that same strength. She believes women can overcome their deepest wounds, forgive, and reclaim the joy and wholeness God has designed for them.

As a leader, author, counselor, and coach, Camille is determined to create safe spaces for healing. She is the founder of the Women Rise Above Club, a movement designed to support women recovering from infidelity and emotional trauma, equipping them with the tools to rebuild and live fulfilling lives.

Her journey is not just about surviving adversity but about transforming it into a ministry that empowers and uplifts others. Through her writing, speaking, and coaching, Camille Fender continues to inspire women everywhere to rise, heal, and walk in their authentic purpose. Also, the author of "Women Rise Above 21 Days Prayer and Fasting Journal" found on Amazon.

Professional Services

Camille Fender is a sought-after speaker, coach, and counselor who delivers powerful insights, faith-driven strategies, and practical wisdom for lasting transformation. She works with individuals, couples, churches, and organizations to bring clarity, healing, and empowerment.

1. **Counseling and Coaching**

    - One-on-one coaching sessions for personal growth and healing.

- Marriage and relationship coaching with a focus on communication, trust, and renewal.
- Infidelity recovery and resilience-building programs.

2. **Speaking Engagements and Workshops**

- Keynote addresses at conferences, churches, and women's events.
- Interactive workshops on infidelity recovery, marriage empowerment, and emotional healing.
- Motivational talks on resilience, purpose, and faith-driven transformation.

3. **Faith-Based Development**

- Group mentorship programs rooted in biblical principles.
- Empowerment sessions to strengthen emotional, spiritual, and relational health.

Speaking Topics

✓ Healing from Infidelity and Broken Trust
✓ The Power and Benefits of Forgiveness
✓ Marriage and Relationship Empowerment
✓ Overcoming Emotional Wounds
✓ Faith-Based Personal Growth

Contact Information

Phone: (876) 362-8302

Email: camillektyrell@gmail.com

Instagram and TikTok: @Camille_fender

Facebook: Camille Fender

For counseling, coaching, workshops, or speaking engagements, book Camille Fender today and take the first step toward healing, empowerment, and transformation.

www.ingramcontent.com/pod-product-compliance
Lightning Source LLC
LaVergne TN
LVHW010931110826
845149LV00013B/2553